THE SKY WATCHED

POEMS OF OJIBWE LIVES

Linda LeGarde Grover

Linda LeGarde Grover

© 2015 Linda LeGarde Grover
Cover photograph and design © 2015 Susan Gardner
© Author's photograph by Brett Groehler, 2015, used by permission.

All rights reserved. No part of this book may be reproduced in any form, by any means, electronic or mechanical, without permission in writing from the author, except for brief quotations for the purpose of reviews.

"Lost and astigmatic 29-year-old self" *Yellow Medicine Review: A Journal of Indigenous Literature, Art and Thought*, Southwest Minnesota State University Fall 2015. "Redemption" *The Cambridge History of American Poetry*, A. Bendixen and S. Burt, editors. Cambridge University Press, 2014. "Parturition: A Poem for Brenda" "The Beanbag" *Migrations: Prose and Poetry for Life's Transitions*, Wildwood River Press, 2011. "Everything You Need to Know in Life You'll Learn at Boarding School" "South Dakota Mission School, 1890" "Leaving" "Mat at Home" "Bemidji" "Grandmother at Indian School" "Lights Out" "Lugalette" "Bernadette" "Bruneaux" "Mary Remembering on a July Afternoon" "Order" "Town, As I Recall It" "Escape" "Chi Ko-ko-koho and the Boarding School Prefict, 1934" "Miss Shawn" "For Asin" "The Class of 1968" "To the Woman Who Just Bought a Set of Native American Spirituality Dream Interpretation Cards" "Mary Susan" "The Refugees" THE.INDIAN.AT.INDIAN.SCHOOL, University of Arkansas at Little Rock, 2009. "Nindaaniss Waawaashkeshikwesens on a Winter Night" "Redemption" *Trail Guide to the Northland Experience in Prints and Poetry*, Calyx Press, 2008. "Anishinaabikwe-Everywoman" *Wind, Dust & Fire*, Bemidji State University, Spring 2007. "Winona Conceives the Trickster" "The Beanbag" "Parturition" *Yellow Medicine Review: A Journal of Indigenous Literature, Art and Thought*, Southwest Minnesota State University, Winter 2007. "Grandmother at Indian School" "St. Bernard" "Everything You Need to Know in Life You'll Learn at Boarding School" "To the Woman Who Just Bought That Set of Native American Spirituality Dream Interpretation Cards" "Nindaaniss Waawaashkeshikwesens on a Winter Night" "Chi-ko-ko-ho and the Boarding School Prefect" "Redemption" "The Refugees" *Traces in Blood, Bone and Stone: Contemporary Ojibwe Poetry*, Loonfeather Press, 2006. "Ma at Home" "Everything You Need to Know in Life You'll Learn at Boarding School" "Leaving" *North Coast Review* No. 22, 2003. "To the Woman Who Just Bought That Set of Native American Spirituality Dream Interpretation Cards" "Ikwe Ishpeming" "Chi Ko-ko-ho and the Boarding School Prefect" *Sister Nations*, Minnesota Historical Society Press, 2002. "Migwechiwendam" "Migwechiwendam Shaaganaashiimowin" "Redemption" *Flight Scape: A Multi-Directional Collection of Indigenous Writings*, Theytus Books 2001. "The Refugees" *pha'atitude Literary Magazine*, November 2001. "The Girls of Casualty Days" *The Roaring Muse*, Department of English, University of Minnesota Duluth, Spring 2001. Nindaaniss Waawaashkeshikwesens on a Winter Night" "My Dad, Who Treats Life Like a Sacrament" *My Home As I Remember*, Natural Heritage Books, 2000. "Lost and astigmatic 29-year-old self" *Yellow Medicine Review: A Journal of Indigenous Literature, Art and Thought*, Southwest Minnesota State University Fall 2015

ISBN 978-0-9908047-7-2
Printed in the United States of America

RED MOUNTAIN PRESS
Santa Fe, New Mexico · www.redmountainpress.us

To my daughters: Waaboosoons, Giizis and Waawaashkeshi

and to my sister Susie

Winters she became the sun, summers the moon.

With thanks to my husband, Tim. "Did you see the new kid?" my girlfriend asked on the first day of eleventh grade. How lucky for me that I turned to look. Migwech for so many things, among them your good-hearted willingness to read and reread my work.

And with thanks to Red Mountain Press. Migwech to Susan Gardner and Devon Ross for your grace and patience, your humor and candor, and your gifts of time and company.

I ZIIGWAN SPRING	7
Redemption	9
Winona Conceives the Trickster	11
Windigo Bimose	12
II NIIBIN SUMMER	15
Everything You Need to Know in Life	17
You'll Learn at Boarding School	17
The Story of Victoria and Elias	18
South Dakota Mission School, 1890	20
Leaving	22
Ma at Home	24
Bemidji	25
Grandmother at Indian School	27
The Canticle of the Night	28
Saint Bernard	29
Lugalette	30
Bernadette	31
Bruneaux	32
Mary Remembering, on a July Afternoon	33
Order	35
Town, As I Recall It	38
Escape	40
Chi Ko-ko-koho and the Boarding School Prefect, 1934	42
III DAGWAAGIN AUTUMN	45
Lost and Astigmatic Twenty-Nine-Year-Old Self	47
The Refugees	49
Mewinzhaa, Bijiinaago Marie and Uncle Roy	51
The Invisible Child	52
Miss Shawn	53
For Asin	55
The Class of 1968	57
Lisa, Let Us Remember Richard	58
To the Woman Who Just Bought That Set of Native American Spirituality Dream Interpretation Cards	61
Mary Susan	63
Nindaaniss Waawashkeshikwesens On A Winter Night	64
My Dad, Who Treats Life Like a Sacrament	65
IV BIBOON WINTER	67
Anishinaabikwe - Everywoman	69
Ikwe Ishpiming	70
Casualty Days	71
Parturition, a Poem for Brenda and Terrie	74
The Beanbag	76
Looking for a Woman with the Blues	78
Setting Bait for the Trickster	79
E.W. Bohannon, My Grandmother, and Me	80
Magdalene in the Shade of Veronica's Love	82
Migwechiwendam Ojibwemowin	83
Migwechiwendam Shaaganaashimowin	84

I ZIIGWAN SPRING

Redemption

After the Great Flood and long before the memory of mortals, Nanaboozhoo and four animals floated on a raft looking for a surface upon which they could live and walk. Amik (Beaver), Ojig (Fisher), and Nigiig (Otter) each exhausted their strengths diving to find where the ground originated, but they were unable to stay underwater long enough to find the bottom. As they despaired, the last and smallest animal, Wazhashk (Muskrat) asked to take a turn. Nanaboozhoo and the other animals told him that it was hopeless and not to try, but the muskrat insisted. It is because of the courage and sacrifice of Wazhashk that the earth was renewed.

Wazhashk, the sky watched this.
Mewinzhaa, long before the memory of mortals
Wazhashk, the sky watched your timid, gallant warrior body
     deliberate and then plunge
         with odd grace and dreadful fragility
    into translucent black water,
      dark mystery unknown and vast as the night sky
and barely - to a single inhalation shared by a weeping four
and a hopeful splash quieter than an oar - break the surface
     into concentric expanding disappearing rings as
     water circled your departure,
     for a moment transparently covering
     rose-gray soles tiny seed pearl toes
     above that determined small warrior body
     that hurtled from sight then
     in an instant was pulled into cold dark depths,
     seeking the finite in the veins of a waterlocked earth.

Wazhashk, the water covering the earth watched this.
Mewinzhaa, long before the memory of mortals
 Wazhashk, when you were obscured from the sky
the water watched you
     lost from the sight of the praying four
     alone on a small raft afloat on vast water
nearly faint under crushing cold
     alone then below the waterline
     seeking the finite in the veins of a cumbrous earth
     as waterfingers intruded and invaded
     all unguarded aspects of your small warrior body
     now stiff and graceless, pulled by will
     into icy dark depths.

Wazhashk, in that dark mystery
unknown and vast as the night sky
you continued your solitary plunge
        lost from the sight of all who lived above water,
        who considered your size and your courage
until in cold and exhaustion your silent voice whispered
        ningosh nindakamj
        nindayekoz niwiinibaa
        I am frightened I am cold
        I am tired I must sleep now
and was heard by the Great Spirit.

Wazhashk, you were heard and were answered
        mangide'en, anamiindim mangide'en
        gaawiin gimbezhigo siin
        anamiindim mangide'en
        have courage, have courage in the depths
        you are not alone
        have courage, have courage in the depths
til your spirit roused and spoke
        geget geget
        through my despair I will

and the Great Spirit watched this and guided you.
Mewinzhaa, long before the memory of mortals,
Wazhashk, the Great Spirit guided you and watched
        your small curled brown fingers
        stretch their curving pink-nailed claws
        to grasp the muddy, rocky breast
        of a waiting Mother Earth.

And today, Wazhashk, hear us breathe
our inhalations and exhalations a continuing song
of courage sacrifice grace redemption a continuing song
since long before the memory of mortals.

With each telling of the story with each singing of the song
        we once again rise to break the surface and seek
        the finite beyond the grace of this merciful Earth
        the finite beyond the mercy of this graceful Earth.

Winona Conceives the Trickster

Mewinzhaa, a long time ago, before she became Nokomis, grandmother of Nanaboozhoo, the moon's most beloved daughter was envied by her sisters the stars, who tricked her into falling to earth from their home, the sky. She gave birth to a daughter, Winona, who she sheltered carefully, wishing to protect her from all harm and danger; however, Winona strayed from her mother while they were out digging potatoes. She was captured in a violent whirlwind by the North Wind, and became pregnant. Nokomis, who grieved terribly when her daughter died in childbirth, raised her grandson Nanaboozhoo with patience and wisdom.

Trees whistle a warning and look to the sky

as shivering stones dance in liquid blue field

and listening moccasins warily step

soft up, soft up and a turn, then freeze

as the North Wind seizes the night.

An ice snake winds past Old Woman Moon

his cloudless stealth feinting gusts of breath

and shocked stars rue their jealous past

watching First Daughter spin on the edge of the world

as the North Wind takes the night.

Windigo Bimose

At the end of that last summer
    that last summer we were like you
when even the pines could give us no shade
and their brown, sharp needles, paler each day, fell
    at first I thought the sound was rain
and lay lifeless where they fell,
where they cut and scratched our feet 'til they swelled

at the time of day that no shadows were cast
a piece of fire fell from the sky
and the sun grew on the ground.
Ravenous, it began to eat the earth.

Carrying babies, grandparents, the infirm
we fled, for a time ahead of the smoke and flames
but after the dry hungry summer
we were in a weakened state, even
the strongest. One by one we made the choice
to continue alone or die with our families;
    I cannot fault one's decision to stay
    or another's to abandon
for myself, after my old parents, my wife
and our children all but one fell like pine needles
I chose to walk with my firstborn.

My oldest daughter who'd always been
strong as a man and slow to tire
walked beside me for how long
    days, nights, lifetimes.

When she tripped and fell, the others
    fewer in number
    than the fingers on both my hands
watched without hope or interest
    would I have done the same if I were them
her struggle to stand, singed lids closing
slowly slowly over dulled desiccated eyes.

As I lifted my firstborn my heart recalled
        her birth, her mother
        her small brothers and sisters
        her grandparents
and tore. Rent, it spilled and emptied.

Then from the void my hunger emerged
        much like the sun's
and through the air less smoky now I smelled
from the north a corporal warmth
        a young mother's arms and breast
and heard from the north a lost child's cry
        young bones and skin tender
        ice-cut feet bleeding into snow

Follow me; let us walk, I said to the others.

Ravenous, I lifted my daughter.
Ravenous, I carried her across my shoulders.
Ravenous, I stepped the first step
        follow me; let us walk
and then ravenous, the remnant rose and followed.

We had fled from heat to live in the cold,
endless cold our dark and everlasting life
where we never slept again, and where
in endless appetite we search for you
        your warm breath
        your blood that flows bright and steams
        in icy winter air
        how we despise your frailties, envy your strengths
        how we love and hate your living flesh

how we yearn and crave past death
past life we hunger, and we walk today.

II NIIBIN SUMMER

Everything You Need to Know in Life You'll Learn at Boarding School

Speak English. Forget the language of your grandparents. It is dead. Forget their teachings. They are ignorant and unGodly. Cleanliness is next to Godliness. Indians are not clean. Your mother did not teach you to be clean. Stand in line. You will learn cleanliness. This is a toothbrush. Hang it on the hook next to the others. Do not allow the bristles to touch. This spreads the disease that you bring to school from your families. Make your bed with mitered corners. A bed not properly made will be torn apart. Start over. Remember and be grateful that the boarding school feeds and clothes you. Say grace before meals. In English. Do not cry. Crying never solved anything.

Write home once each month. In English.

Tell your mother that you are doing very well. You'll never amount to anything. Answer when the teacher addresses you. In English. We discourage visits from your family. If you visit your family in the summer, report to the matron's office immediately upon your return. You will be allowed into the dormitory after you have been sanitized and de-loused. Busy hands are happy hands. Keep yourself occupied. You'll never amount to anything. Books are our friends. Reading is your key to the world. In English. Forget the language of your grandparents. It is dead. If you are heard speaking it you will kneel on a navy bean for one hour. Do not cry. Crying never solved anything. We will ask if you have learned your lesson. You will answer. In English. Spare the rod and spoil the child. We will not spare the rod. We will cut your hair. We will shame you. We will lock you in the basement. Learn from that. Improve yourself. Speak English. Forget the language of your grandparents. It is dead. You'll never amount to anything.

The Story of Victoria and Elias

Menwinzhaa, ninokomis gaye nimishoomis gii-abinoojiwag.
Long ago, my grandmother and grandfather were children.

Ninokomis gii-zhinikaazo Victoria Ma-Kwe-Mad.
O bii-odabiitoon Onamanii zaga-iganing.
My grandmother was named Victoria Ma-Kwe-Mad.
She lived at Lake Vermilion.

Nimishoomis gii-izhinikaazo Elias LeGarde.
Ogii-odabiitoon Nah-Gah-Chi-Wa-Nong.
My grandfather was named Elias LeGarde.
He lived at Fond du Lac.

Apii Elias gaye Victoria gii-abinoojiyiwaad,
Anishinaabe wi-abinaoojiwag gii-maajiinaawag widi
Gikinoo'amaading wigawigong waasa.
When Elias and Victoria were children,
Anishinaabe children were sent away
from their homes to school.

Elias gaye Victoria oshiimeyiwaan gii-maagiiwanag iwidi
Vermilion gikin'amaading wigamigong.
Elias and Victoria and their brothers and sisters
went away to the Vermilion boarding school.

Apii gii-maajaawaad gii-gigashkendamoog gakina awiya.
Abinoojiwag gii-mawiwag.
When they left everyone was sad.
The children cried.

Elias ogii-zaagi'aan Victoria,
minawaa Victoria obii-zaagi'aan Elias.
Elias loved Victoria,
and Victoria loved Elias.

Apii Elias gaye Victoria giigizhigiiwad, gii wiidigewag.
Gii-izhaawag Onigamiising.
When Elias and Victoria grew up, they got married.
They went to Duluth.

Noongoom, LeGardes odoobiitanawaa Onigamiising.
Noongoom ingiw LeGarde abinoojiwag aanawa endaawaad.
Gikinoo'imawaawag amaadii wigamong Ongamiising imaa..

Noongoom LeGardes maamawi-ayaawag.
Minwendaanawaa dash.
Today the LeGardes live in Duluth.
Today the LeGarde children live at home.
They go to school in Duluth.
Today the LeGardes all live together.
And they are happy.

LeGardes omisawendaanawaa maamawi apane ji-ayaawaad.
The LeGardes will stay together forever.

Onishishin.
That is pretty (good).

South Dakota Mission School, 1890

At mission school so far away from home
at night I heard the song through dreams of trees,
birches and jackpines in rocky woods
that I walked in my white nightgown, peering
through night fog for my mother, who perhaps
might walk in her own dreams, looking for me.

Days inside the classroom, prim and chaste
we kept our dark wool dresses smooth and clean,
covered by starched white aprons bleached
immaculate by our absence of sin
and practiced English by living it,
our lives limited as our proficiency
in that language and our peculiar use of it.

Evenings, Sister Joseph read aloud,
her pale and unlined face benign behind
spectacles that mirrored twin gaslights
while Sister Agnes taught us fancy work,
and so we improved our English by listening
and our skills as ladies by embroidering
handkerchiefs and petticoat hems.

Nights, across the plain we heard them sing,
the foreign Indians, throughout that icy fall.
As winter started, still the people sang
in a language that we didn't understand.
Sister Joseph said to pray for their poor souls,
those Sioux hadn't been blessed with mission school
yet, and didn't speak English.
You'll never be White if you don't try, she said;
I will confess I half-believed I could.
We mission girls had left our pagan ways
behind when we learned how to read and write
and about Jesus, and the sin of our old ways.
We tried to be like his Blessed Mother,
or as close as Christian Chippewa girls could get.
No wicked willfulness here. We had learned
to do as we were told,

which on that winter night we did, although
we didn't understand why, awakened
from light virgin sleeps to stand shivering

beside our narrow white iron beds
by Sister Agnes, who told us to hurry.
Wrapped in blankets pulled off of the beds
and naked under our white nightgowns,
a sight to scandalize the Blessed Mother
we did as we were told,
no wicked willfulness here
and followed Sister outside into the night
through brittle long grass
that cracked under our bare cold feet
to lie in a frozen ditch. Beneath our warmth
sparkling frost patterns on dark earth
melted, turning ice crystals to mud
that smeared shocking stains on our nightgowns
as we did as we were told.
No wicked willfulness here.

From the ravine we heard gunshots, then a keening
that rose so thinly, a sliver of smoke into the sky
and Sister said to lie still, girls, heads down
and she whispered to the Blessed Mother,
"please ask your Son to spare these baptized girls"
who did as they were told.

And what did I think, while
pressed indecently to that frozen muddy ground
as the nightgown of the girl next to me
blew skyward in the icy wind
doing its own ghost dance; did I ask why?
Did I ask for the Blessed Mother's help
and for Jesus to spare the baptized Indians?
Well, I prayed for my mother, and my brother Louis.
>   I prayed to see them again;
>   I prayed for the other girls and for the Sisters
>   for myself, I confess; forgive me
>   and for those foreign Indians the Sioux, God help them
>   for mercy for us all
and then
I prayed in my own language,
my lips open and moving to release no sound
unbound silent words a visible cloud
above ice crystals melting on frozen earth
turning to mud against my body, those words
shades of blue and gray without sound those words
uncoiling winding silent cold
and as determined as the wind.

LEAVING

Old enough now to walk to the depot ourselves,
we waved to Ma
and she smiled back from the porch, waving
> *goodbye! see you in the summer!*
> *take care of your little sister!*
in one breath looking smaller, in another out of sight.

Turning the corner I looked back -
she wiping her eyes on her sleeve,
coarse twilled cotton comfort
drying my tears also, I almost thought,
but it was just the wind blowing cold tracks
that dried to a salty soreness
from the corners of my eyes to my ears
as I blinked in the bright cold sun.

Brud the oldest carried Angeline the youngest
wrapped in her new coat a warm brown
> cut down from her own
> by Ma, for starting school.

It wasn't easy. On the train
Angeline cried herself a hundred miles,
her tears a spring of misery deep as China
while our own dripped down our throats
to our stomachs, sour puddles
that in briny darkness would never dry.

Later, Angeline slept
lulled by the rumble of the train
dulled by the lullaby of grief
her face hot and thin cheeks shiny
from salty runoff, in her dreams
gasping arrhythmic short intakes of breath
that kept me awake. I looked out the window
at the progression of small towns, a movie run backwards
from our trip home last June,
and when it got too dark to see outside
I stayed turned to the window, watching
that familiar reversal of heart's order
reel after reel reflected in the glass
in rehearsal it seemed for our destination,
that life backwards from all we knew at home

Angeline Brud Mitchell and Waboos
sleeping in the glare of the overhead light
a tangle of children smelling home in dreams
as their heads rested on Ma's cut-down coat,
then my own staring face blank, tearless
smooth as stone, reflected in the window
reversed too in the glass and in my senses
in rehearsal it seemed for our destination,
that life backwards from all we knew at home

> *left hand to right daylight to darkness*
> *yes ma'am yes sir raise your head*
> *stand at attention take your beating*
> *remember remember remember*

MA AT HOME

After they turned the corner, that huddle of children
carrying bread to eat on the train, my children
with their dark coats still faces resigned feet
that had walked down the porch stairs
moving, moving, a catch of breath seen and felt

walking forward and away, a catch and a pause
but then forward, forward to the corner
in one breath looking smaller, in another out of sight

>   *goodbye! see you in the summer!*
>   *take care of your little sister!*

I lowered my arm and placed into its crook my smile
and my tears, the full-blown bloom of my heart
damp on a dark cotton dress sleeve.
Back in the house my hands did their tasks
without the summer help of my heart
whose seasons had changed in two beats:
picked up the quilts from the floor, folding
>   gray and black wool, old skirts and trousers
>   bits of red, a man's wool shirt
>   faded maroon and brown, my wedding quilt
>   and the lightest a summer dress, flowers blurred in fog

tucking batting where patches frayed and threads broke
>   smoothing soothing mothering
>   the prints of my children's bodies

to squares that I placed under the bed, until after spring.
Then I walked to work, warm without my coat,
cut down for Angeline, the smallest and today the warmest
walking to the train in her huddle of brothers
in my cut-down coat, my arms around her arms
my shoulders on her shoulders
my cut-down coat warming her in my absence
my smile and wave the last she saw
my starving eyes the last she felt,
on the back of her small head the combed-in line
that parted her hair between her tiny braids.

Small Angeline.
With her brothers she walked, without them I waited,
back to my old hangnail existence, three seasons deadened
but living for the day they would return.

Bemidji

When I tucked my feet under the bench
and looked down, my legs ended at the knees;
no brown high top shoes no black wool stockings
just legs that ended where my knee pants ended.
If I pushed my stomach out to a hard air-filled paunch
my hunger ended at my ribs
no emptiness no growl no sorrow
just an ache in the hollow of nothing to eat.

Passing time we were, my brothers and me
waiting at the bus depot for the priest,
strangers in a strange land. We sat
as straight and quiet as if he watched us
while we watched for him. Waited.

Lethargic homesick patient heartsick
fatigued with the wait and restless,
swinging our feet from the bench, getting up
roaming the block begging bread from a bakery
eating on the sidewalk watching and waiting
for the priest in his black car. It's funny
nobody noticed us but the ticket seller
who ignored us and went home
leaving us to sleep there in the waiting room
on wooden benches slippery as church pews.

Awake in the dark depot that first night
I sat up, then knelt on the seat of the bench,
my mouth resting on the curved back, tasting
and smelling church, sour smell and salt
damp change, soft bills, chewing gum, matchbooks
a tackiness from other people's hands on my lips
as I passed time awake in the dark depot, waiting
for the priest in his black car. It's funny
nobody noticed us, nobody missed us.

The bakery lady fed us twice, children like
cautious squirrels, or timid small birds,
small town wildlife nearly tamed,
carrying that leftover bread back
past the eyes of the passive ticket seller
to our den our nest our chapel the depot
our new life, that brick and concrete waiting room
a purgatory between home and boarding school.

Then that second morning, uneasy though we were
the dread of returning to Indian school lessened
ever so slightly and we began to hope, maybe
we would shine shoes, wash dishes
find lost change on the sidewalk
and we'd buy tickets home from the ticket seller
who wouldn't say, aren't you boys from the Indian school?
And we'd ride home on the bus, walk in the door
and surprise our mother. The second night we dreamed that,
moving and turning easily on our varnished pews
turning in our dreams to look out the bus windows
seeing towns reversed from our trip north
time running backward it seemed
a natural and right progression
(in the misplaced dreams of hopeful boys)
in the hopeful dreams of misplaced boys.

GRANDMOTHER AT INDIAN SCHOOL

Left on scrubbed wooden steps to think
about disobedience, and forgetfulness
she feels warm sun on the back of her neck
as she kneels on the pale spot worn
by other little girls' tender sore knees,
a hundred black wool stockings
grinding skin and stairs,
beneath one knee a hard white navy bean.

Distant lightening flickers and nears,
flashes down her shins, felt by other
uniformed girls marching to sewing class
waiting for their own inevitable return
to the stair, to think and remember what happens
to girls who speak a pagan tongue.

Try to forget this pagan tongue.

Disobedient and forgetful she almost hears
beyond the school yard
beyond the train ride
beyond little girls crying in white iron beds

her mother far away
singing to herself as she cooks
speaking quietly to Grandma as they sew
the quilt for the new baby
and laughing with the aunties
while they wash clothes
    the little bean,
    does it hurt?
Bizaan, gego mawi ken; hush, don't cry
she thinks, moving her knee so the little bean
feels only the soft part, and not the bone
    how long can I stay here?

And when Matron returns to ask if she's thought
she says yes, I won't talk like a pagan again
and she stands and picks up the little bean
and carries it in her lonesome, lying hand
until lights out,
when the baby bean
sleeps under her pillow.

The Canticle of the Night

Under the window a sheet glows
blue, as a little boy breathes
a dream melody, soft snores in and out,
his moonlit skin a lunar lavender.
He turns once, twice, dreams.

Across the room unseen by the moon
the bed in the corner hidden by shadow
creaks, springs an assonant whine
as a restless sleeper kicks a gray wool blanket
from his soaring in the sky to earth.

Five other beds are gray shapes in the night
two lumpy mounds, two barely outlined bodies
the fifth a frightened dreamer who yelps,
flailing union-suited limbs
shadow to moonlight, brown gray blue
below the bright moon rising higher in the sky.

This night two boys wait, breathing in unison
below the cry below the snores
below the whine of bedsprings
below the moon's slow sail through the night.
Turned, their faces are mirrored
one in shadow one in moonlight
counting stars counting snores
counting days weeks years

Their breathing a silent descant
        one more night gone
        one more night
        one more gone
to the canticle of the night.

Saint Bernard

When I got to mission school
my worries about my mother
and how was she doing without me
had to wait when
the priest told me
I had a bigger worry than that.

When I died, he said,
they would never let me into heaven
when they heard my name.

With a name like mine, Barney
not any kind of Bible name at all
I couldn't float in
past the eyes of God.

He'd turn me away for certain
with a name like mine, Barney
and send me back to mission school.

And so they named me after this big dog
who carried whiskey
in a little barrel around his neck
and saved people's lives
by bringing them a drink.

Well, I'd heard about that
and even saw it with my own eyes
in a bar in the West End.
Thanks, niijii, you saved my life
a man told my uncle,
I was sure dying for a drink.

So I supposed it must be all right
and tried to feel the honor
of my namesake.

But it didn't stick
and I reverted to my pagan ways.
See, when I got home
and my mother said hello Barney
I was so happy
I forgot all about heaven.

LUGALETTE

One thing we never had at school was lugalette.
I always thought that word sounded so funny, LUGGLE-ett.
Some of the kids at school called it lug-o-lay, and some called it
Indian bread or lug bread or just plain lug,
but they all knew what it was.

Back at home we had it every day, lugalette.
"What are you cooking, Ma?" I would ask
just to hear her say "lugalette" and laugh.

Here's how you make lugalette.
Take enough flour to fill a good-size bowl about half full
and mix in just a small handful of baking powder, some salt,
a bigger handful of sugar. Then draw a circle in it, to make a
little river, and mix in enough warm water or milk to make a
nice soft dough. Knead the dough just a little, let it rest a little
bit, then put it in a greased pan and flatten it, careful, with your
hands. Bake it twenty, thirty minutes.

Some people cut the lugalette into squares before they bake it,
cut it into squares right in the pan, that makes it easier to break
into pieces after it's cooked. My mother used to slice it. You
can eat it hot or cold. If you've got some blueberries, you can
mix a handful into the dough, and that's good, too.
Mino pagwad.

Back at home our mother made it every day.
I always wished for it.
We never had it at school, lugalette.

BERNADETTE

My first night at boarding school
the girl next to me in the dormitory
talked in Indian to me, asked me
just like the people at home
where I was from and who my family was
which comforted me. Then she said
don't wash your stockings yet;
we need the radiators.
The girls took out the bread
they'd saved from supper, and a jar of syrup
and said they were having a party for me,
the new girl. I'd never had a party before.

They taught me to make zip sandwiches.
Have you heard of them, zip sandwiches?
You take a piece of bread and pour a little syrup
and fold it and let it heat up and dry out
flat and hard on the radiator. Zip sandwiches.

Next time there was a new girl
sitting all sad and lonesome on her bed
I said after the matron was gone
"Aniin, ezhiyaa yayaan?"
and told her to save her bread from supper
for a party that night. She smiled sideways.

Those zip sandwiches? Hard, stiff, sticky they were
a little unsanitary for my taste, drying out
right where we would hang our underwear
after we washed it in the sink.
And flavor? Well, they didn't have much
but we loved them, and to this day, to me
when I eat any sweet, stiff, sticky food
it makes me think of those days,
and I taste kindness, and comfort,
the goodness and generosity of those girls.

BRUNEAUX

It was a good job.
Close to town. Regular pay.
Room and board. A good job.

Don't look at me, I wasn't the first one;
other Shinnobs had done it before me
and all things considered I didn't mind it
even if it was at a goddam Indian school.

The boys? They were all right, the boys,
and we all got along when they kept their noses clean.
And when they didn't, there wasn't anything new,
nothing I didn't see before, those hellish days
I was a boy at Indian school, myself.
Runaways fighters young
blanket-ass Indians sneaking around
like their ceremonies were a big secret from me
talking Indian under their breaths
like I couldn't understand what they were saying.
I took care of all that,
and when I caught some of them
having a little Indian dance out in the woods
I took care of that, too.

Every one that I beat
the ones who cried and the silent ones
the ones who broke
the ones who disappeared into themselves
they all acted like I didn't know myself
what a beating was. What did they think,
that I was born knowing how?
I went to goddam Indian school, too.

Mary Remembering, on a July Afternoon

An afternoon like this reminds me of my grandma,
when she taught us how to bead
one summer. On a day like today, warm.
Summers she wore a gray cotton dress
washed so soft and light it fluttered
when she walked. On a day like today, warm
she stretched carpet thread on a wooden loom,
ignoring dishes, laundry, ironing,
chores that could wait, those afternoons
that flowers grew beneath my grandma's hands.
Rough knuckles she had and long-boned fingers
that lifted beads carefully from a jar lid
with her needle counting
two blue two red eight white two red four green
four white four green two blue six white two blue.
A steamy afternoon it was at the table
where she sat flanked and squeezed
by me and Cynthia getting closer and closer
as we watched, pressing against her sides
yet she never said to move away it was too hot;
only that the warm breath from our open mouths
limbered her fingers, softened the beeswax
with which she coated the thread,
and gave her a good grip on the sticky loom.

One day she gave us little wooden looms
she'd made, and our own needles, fast and silvery
to try out beading, and we felt honored
to do what Grandma did; honored
we watched and did what she did.
Threaded our looms
picked up beads with our needles
pressed up and wove
into no pattern at all, just beads,
but you know? She praised us,
praised us anyway, said that looks good.

It's been eighty years since I saw my Grandma
but I remember when we learned to bead,
when flowers grew and bloomed beneath her hands
that summer just before my father died.

Mother in her sadness never sang
again, spending nights drinking, days asleep
til the Indian agent noticed and sent me
to boarding school, where I was to forget
what Grandma taught me, and learn other ways.

But, I remembered when we learned to bead
that summer flowers grew beneath her hands
and when we brought our bracelets to town,
a long, hot walk with Grandma to the store.
We sold our "just beads" bracelets for ten cents,
and Grandma got a dollar each for hers.
She said, you girls keep your money,
and bought blue yarn, brown sugar,
white cheesecloth and three red suckers
for the long walk home, purchased
along with endless days, I would have thought,
of Mother singing as she sewed and cooked
of Father cutting pulp and hauling scrap
and Grandma, flanked and squeezed by two small girls
who watched her work.

                    I never did forget
that summer when she taught us how to bead,
when flowers grew and bloomed beneath her hands
and held it in my heart those lonely days
at school. Marching to class learning English
scrubbing the floors I held it in my heart,
that summer when she taught us how to bead,
those brown fingers, that soft gray dress, the steam
from summer heat, and learning-breathing mouths
limbering her fingers and the threads,
that summer Grandma taught us how to bead.

ORDER

Bells at six.
Wash face and hands.
Brush teeth.
Hang the toothbrush on the hook with your initials next to it.
Gather clean stockings and underclothes from the radiator
school dress and apron from the hook on the wall
shoes from under the bed.
Air the bed.
Dress.
Comb, part, braid each other's hair.

Bells at six-thirty.
Line up.
March to the dining room.
Stand behind your chair.
At the signal, sit.
At the signal, pray.
At the signal, eat. Oatmeal. Coffee.
At the signal, rise. Line up. File out.
Place dirty dishes in the washtub next to the door.

Bells at seven.
Return to the dormitory.
Make bed.
Sweep.
Dust.

Bells at eight.
Line up.
March to the classroom.
Stand next to your desk.
At the signal, sit.
Lessons. Reading. Writing. Arithmetic. Penmanship.

Bells at eleven-thirty.
Line up.
March to the dining room.
Stand behind your chair.
At the signal, sit.
At the signal, pray.
At the signal, eat. Soup. Bread. Milk.
At the signal, line up. File out.
Places dirty dishes in the washtub next to the door.

Bells at twelve-thirty.
Line up.
March to the dormitory.
Change into ticking-stripe work dress.
Hang school dress and apron on the hook next to the bed.

Bells at one.
Line up.
March to work.
Mondays, laundry.
Tuesdays, mending.
Wednesdays, ironing.
Thursdays, floors.
Friday, sewing.

Bells at four-thirty.
Line up.
March to the dining room.
Stand behind your chair.
At the signal, sit.
At the signal, pray.
At the signal, eat. Beans. Potatoes. Bread. Blanc mange. Coffee.
At the signal, line up. File out.
Place dirty dishes in the washtub next to the door.

Bells at six.
Line up.
March to recreation.
Mondays, reading and letter writing.
Tuesdays, brisk walk around the school grounds.
Wednesdays, reading and letter writing.
Thursdays, brisk walk around the school grounds.
Fridays, dining room for group singing.

Bells at seven-thirty.
Line up.
March to the dormitory. Supervised free time
>   *Meni, you going home this summer?*
>   *Louisa lemme rat your hair for you,*
>   *put it up, like the white girls in town.*
>   *Somebody help Zenta polish her shoes.*

Bells at nine.
Change into nightgown.
Hang work dress on the hook next to the bed.
Place shoes under bed.
Wash underclothes and stockings in the lavatory sink,
hang them on the radiator to dry.
Wash.
Brush teeth.
Hang the toothbrush on the hook with your initials next to it.

Bells at nine-thirty.
Stand next to your bed.
At the signal, kneel.
At the signal, pray.
At the signal, into bed.
Lights out.
Silence.

Listen to the girl in the next bed cry.

Town, As I Recall It

Those Saturdays we got a ride in the wagon from school
with our outing pay, sometimes two, three dollars
in our pockets, a lot of money in those days.

Mabel and me, we never looked at each other
but we were an item and I could see
she had curled the sides of her hair for the occasion.
I'd borrowed my brother's good pants; she could see that
though we never looked at each other.
In town we walked around together
looking in the store windows picking out things we liked.
We were an item, like I said. Once we almost touched
by accident, on my part. Mabel blushed
and looked at her shoes.

We went to school half-days and worked half-days.
Outing they called it, or working out. Me, I worked
for a farmer who liked me; I was a hard worker
and big. He called me "Buck" and let me drive his tractor
a skittish thing wilder than a steer and a lot to handle
rough riding on those iron tires but I enjoyed it.
When I got my money I wanted to buy something for Mabel
who worked out as a mother's helper cleaning their house
wiping their kids' noses scrubbing laundry with a washboard
and their kitchen floors with a brush,
always with chapped hands.
They called it "working out" though she worked "in"
and she never made the kind of money I did.

In the store Mabel bought crochet thread
and I bought her a hair ribbon blue as the sky
because I knew she liked pretty things,
then I mailed a dollar to my mother.

We went to the show and sat in the dark
Mabel and me never touching, yet
across four inches of space and through
the papery starched whiteness of her blouse
I knew
      how did I know
the tenderness of her carbolic-scented skin

cool tender Mabel whose resting fingers curved
in her lap around an invisible scrub brush
so bashful she looked straight at the screen
and obliquely past my eyes
to my hopeful aching self.

I remembered this after I left school
and during the war I remembered this
sitting in the dark with Mabel
inches from her gingery carbolic fragrance
watching the stagecoach make its way west

thinking one day I'd be like John Wayne
the Ringo Kid escaping jail for a better life
with the girl he would save from the bad guys

while Mabel in her starched white blouse
cool tender carbolic-perfumed Mabel
resting fingers curved in her lap
around an invisible scrub brush
as Kid and the Indians traded shots
half smiled in the sweet darkness.

A pretty interesting place to be.
Town.

ESCAPE

There were certain things you could do to leave school.

Finish. Once you finished school you could leave. Most didn't finish but some did. Some went on to another boarding school for high school or to learn a trade. Some stayed on at school and worked there awhile to earn train fare home, or because they didn't know what else to do.

Run away. Runaways and boarding schools always went together; you hear them mentioned together. A lot of kids tried it; a lot were caught. Runaways were easy to find, because they all ran to the same place, home. Some the schools just let run without pursuit for a few days or a week, knowing where to find them. When some of those kids arrived home they were met at the door by someone from school who had been waiting for them. This saved everyone a lot of work. Some kids, though just a few, ran home and never went back to school, either because home was too far away for retrieval to be worth the chase, or because they ran so many times the school got tired of the trouble.

Get sick. There was sickness at boarding school, that's for sure, and at every school. Measles, whooping cough, impetigo all went through the schools and spread. Diphtheria. Influenza. Children sickened, recovered, sickened. The Spanish Flu closed whole schools down in 1918. Trachoma wouldn't get you home, though you might get transferred to a trachoma school. You'd walk around with sore eyes all red and runny; you couldn't see straight. It blinded you, eventually. T.B., tuberculosis, would get you out of school, but you'd go to a sanitarium for your lungs to dry out and scar over.

And that's if you were lucky.
If you weren't, you might be sent home
to give it to your family,
to cough and hemorrhage yourself to death.

Die. You could die from getting sick, or you could die from getting hurt. Accidents, sometimes. There were runaways who died from exposure, or injuries. How many ways to die. A boy kicked downstairs by the disciplinarian; another boy from pneumonia after he wasn't allowed to sleep inside. A little girl with scarlet fever. A teenage girl giving birth in the infirmary. A boy drowned swimming in the lake. Some died from broken hearts; they were just too sad and homesick to eat and couldn't live without their mothers.

CHI KO-KO-KOHO AND THE BOARDING SCHOOL PREFECT, 1934

From this owl's nest home, unsteady greasy oak
covered by cowhide long oblivious
to claws tough and curving as old tree roots
I breathe the night breeze, starry broken glass.

I am Cho Ko-ko-koho. My black-centered
unblinking owl eyes see past the dark
growl of this old bear den of a bar
through a stinging fog of unintended
blasphemy, tobacco's tarry prayers
stuck and dusty on a hammered tin ceiling
to grieving spirits mirrored by my own.

I am Chi Ko-ko-koho, young among owls
as young among lush crimson blooms of death
is the embryonic seedling in my chest
the rooting zygote corkscrew in my chest
these days all but unseen, a pink seaspray
sunset on a thick white coffee cup.
My grieving spirit hardly notices,
though, in this old bear den of a bar.

My owl head turns clear round when I see him.
I am Chi Ko-ko-koho; I blink away
smoke and fog, my head swivels back
and he's still there, the prefect. Still there
and he's real, not some ghost back to grab my throat
again with those heavy no-hands of his
or crack my brother's homesick skinny bones
on cold concrete tattooed by miseries
of other Indian boys who crossed his path.

To the darkness of this bear den of a bar
he's brought his own sad spirit for a drink.

I am Ch Ko-ko-koho, but who he sees
is Kwiiwizens, a boy bent and kneeling
beneath the prefect's doubled leather strap
and Kwiiwizens I am. My belly feels
a tiny worm the color of the moon
writhe in laughter at my cowardice
as that now embodied ghost the old prefect
step-drags step-drags his dampened moccasins

to my end of the bar. Flowers weep rain
and unstrung beads in mourning for us all.

He asks me for a nickel for a beer.

With closed eyes Kwiiwizens waits for the strap
and I see them, the boy and the owl who are me.

Ch Ko-ko-koho dives from his grimy perch
to yank the apparition by the hair,
then flies him past the blind side of the moon
to drop him in the alley back behind
the dark growl of this old bear den of a bar.

Indizhinikaaz Kwiiwizens,
gaye indizhinikaaz Chi Ko-ko-koho.
Ni maajaa. Mi-iw. I leave him there.

I am Chi Ko-ko-koho. I leave him there

under stars of broken glass. I leave him there.

III DAGWAAGIN AUTUMN

LOST AND ASTIGMATIC TWENTY-NINE-YEAR-OLD SELF

As the sign on the door says
printed in bright green crayon on cardboard

    YOU ARE HERE
    SOBRIETY POWWOW
    EVERYBODY WELCOME

and here you are indeed
in 1979, in Onigamiising
in a Methodist church social hall
with your father, who
hearing the drum and singing, brightens
and your three little girls
in matching denim bib overalls and ironed, ruffled blouses.
Here you are

    YOU ARE HERE

squinting at an unclear world from behind thick lenses
(the world will focus in time, but how can you know this,
 twenty-nine-year lost and astigmatic self?)
holding your smallest child's hand and your father's arm

at a sobriety celebration gathering
under institutional fluorescent light fixtures
that on this overcast afternoon
mimic the paleness of the sun glowing through clouds.

As there is beauty
in the pallid light of sun shining through clouds
so there is beauty
in the touching mimicry of the fluorescent lights
in the feast of Indian hot dogs, wild rice, jello, cake,
powdered orange drink and coffee coffee coffee
in the dancers, some in street clothes
some in Indian clothes (as we called them in 1979)
all there in honor of the sobriety warriors
and the warriors, themselves, proud
modest battle-scarred ogichidaa spirits
a little embarrassed by the attention
and the old man who called to my dad
"Jerry LeGarde!"
then spoke to him in Indian

(my dad replied and they conversed,
to my surprise; I didn't know he could do that
and perhaps this is as long and familiar a story
to you as it is to me; if not I will explain sometime)
and the lineup for the food, with the Elders eating first
and Grand Entry, the prayers, the Veterans Song
and the m.c. who made everybody laugh
after a really good song,
so good that everybody in the room got up to dance.

"That was an old traditional song of our people
called 'When I Get My Payment'!"
he announced into the mic,
Indianishly (as we said in 1979)
tempering (as we still do)
extremes of happiness sadness
light and darkness, ugliness and beauty
and the inevitably increasing clarity that each day brings
with a joke.

Lost and astigmatic twenty-nine-year-old self,
the directions you sought were printed in bright green crayon
taped to the doors of a church social hall

>	YOU ARE HERE
>	SOBRIETY POWWOW
>	EVERYBODY WELCOME

There you were
and here you are.

.

THE REFUGEES

To the dirging of "The Way We Were"
sung by some sweet girl nobody knows
six pallbearers
two in sweatshirts with washed away logos
three in second-hand dress shirts
one in a borrowed sportcoat
carry above their bowlegged lockstep mince
the flocked vinyl coffin out the side door. Inside
our beloved mother, grandma and aunt rests,
megis shell on a black string
wound over her bent brown fingers.

Six pallbearers worn as their boot heels
and ground to unassuming humility
by the rounds of looking for work
and sometimes finding it bravely
wear their bodies as a single suit of clothes
fraying fast and worn at the knees.
These are faces of outside work, aging young skin
tanned by the sun and creased
ever more deeply season to season
filled and emptied filled and emptied
with grime and hard living that
search then escape what they've found
spending night after numb night on a stool at Mr. J's
thinking, maybe after one more
I'll ask that blonde or her friend to dance;
no, guess I'll just go home, after all.

This is what really happened to the other Indians,
not the noble savage beauties you watch
on made-for-TV movies, running in crisp, freshly ironed
loincloths through a pristine forest full of friendly animals
with an important message for the Chief
from his daughter the Princess,
who enthrall you so with their simple ways
(*"oh wow these people are just so close to nature,
to SPEAR-itual (I wannabe, I wanna have)"*
that you can buy at a craft show stand
along with some gen-yew-whine turquoise and silver
jewelry so that you can be an Indian, too.

No, we're the other Indians,
the ones who did our time in boarding school
where we learned to take a beating
never quite mastered forced English
learned the work ethic and what it meant for us
but survived, more or less, in spite of it.

We moved to town, refugees we became
displaced persons scorned by our own people.
Our daughters married white men
and learned to take a beating
never quite mastered Anglo housekeeping
lived the work ethic and for them it meant
they would grow old early *our daughters*
beloved and revered the bearers of life
and generations to come how could we protect them,
our daughters whose spirits tired and whose
blue-eyed children went to public school
and learned to take a beating
as well as give one in return
never mastered school work,
leaving when they turned sixteen,
having learned what the work ethic meant for them
so they too could live hard and grow old early.

And today we're at another funeral,
and since it's the mortuary's rock bottom budget
package deal we move outside the Sunset Chapel
once our hour is up. We're grateful
for this warm and sunny day
and for room on the sidewalk
for cousins to meet and talk
("ain't seen you since the last funeral")
til the chapel needs the sidewalk back
and we head for Mr. J's.

Our beloved is gone she has traveled
her four day spirit walk
and has arrived west.
Her corpse waits in a flocked vinyl coffin
on a shelf in the mortuary's garage
for the off-hours ride to the cemetery,
megis shell on a black string
wound over her bent brown fingers.

MEWINZHAA, BIJIINAAGO MARIE AND UNCLE ROY

>(walks in the front door, cracked dark varnish beads around an oval glass. hangs her coat on the stairpost. her mother says here, bring this to your Uncle Roy. carries a plate of buttered soda crackers to the table. watches him pour soup from the tin saucepan into the pink flowered bowl for her, the chipped green one for himself. two spoons. he gives her the shiny one.)

"When I went to school we didn't walk home for dinnertime."

"Did you live too far away?"

"Stayed there for suppertime, too."

>(train ride. lye soap. penmanship. blots and a ruler to bruised knuckles. no tears. loading hay with a pitchfork. Zane Grey in the reading room. a box of cookies from a missionary on Christmas Day. a visit from ma and the old man, unbearable joy in a muted practiced handshake. speaking English, Zhaaganaashiimowin. hello sir, hello mother, we have been very well here)

"We lived at the school."

>(she is too small to know this)

"It was a different kind of school."

>(curiosity) (?) (she lifts his rain-dampened plaid wool jacket from the back of the kitchen chair and drapes it over the radiator to dry)

"Want some more soup?"

>(love for a small girl with short braids)

The Invisible Child

Teacher, I'm quiet here at my desk
looking down you think at
an empty lined worksheet,
my chapped fingers with bitten nails
holding a pencil that's lost its eraser
so I can't make mistakes, and I'm no trouble to you
at all, hiding behind a white girl in a pretty dress.

You don't see my spirit leave this desk
to fly like a bat out of hell through the halls
rehearsing cannonballs, loop-the-loops, skyrockets
for the day you might see me, when I become real
the day I find the updraft and really do fly.

I'm undersized and quiet, mousy you think
and it irritates you to see me puffing my mouse cheeks
while I read at my desk. You don't know it's my teeth
my teeth a painsong accompanying what I do
      when they hurt too much I get one pulled
      and the nails in my shoes rise into my heels
      and my wash-worn socks fall into my shoes
      all winter my cold makes me talk so kids laugh
      and my family's so big you make jokes about us
right at me and I don't get it, teacher.
Don't know what sex is or birth control but I know it's a joke.
Sometimes I laugh too so you can't see
my ten-year-old feelings hurt, but you can't see.

Teacher, who's more ignorant, you or me?

I'm quiet and undersized and no trouble at all,
behind that girl in the pretty dress. Watching your world
I listen to you and think about you too
as my spirit flies like a bat through the halls
unseen, teacher, unseen until the day I become real
the day I find the updraft and really do fly.

MISS SHAWN

I am afraid of that deceptive face
        handsome dark-eyed intelligent
        in structure a sheep's face or a camel's
        with an animal's acceptance and dignity
        that masks a cruel soul I have seen before
but even more of that melodic voice
a deep and long-vowelled cello song oozing
through a beige throat draped by long folds of skin
two knobs at its fearsome base, and to its
menacing and oddly tuneful hypnotic beat
"Linda LeGarde" I rise as learned the hard way
to stand at the right side of the desk
eyes front straight ahead face to face with Miss Shawn
chilled by the meter of that voice
my left hand touching home, my desk
fixed and stable, warm wood with floral iron grillwork
a trellised passage to the tranquility and safety
of sitting behind the boy who blocks her view of me
but I have risen now and stand exposed
eyes front straight ahead face to face with Miss Shawn.

"Your family is Indian. What tribe are you people from?"

And while above thirty-three other iron-trellised desks
pale faces turn to watch the glare of my misery
curious and glad it's not them
the other Indian child in class looks away,
sympathetic and sorry it's my turn. He knows;
he's had more than his share. I stand exposed
in need of cover
        try not to look afraid
eyes front straight ahead face to face with Miss Shawn
        and can't look down, that's not allowed
as she takes two steps and I can't help it
my eyes drop and I can see it all so clearly.

Brown leather teacher shoes with chunky heels. Two extra
pairs on the shelf by her desk. Brown teacher dress, chunky pin
over the left breast. More teacher dresses gray beige maroon in
her closet at home. Teacher car in the parking lot, tan Chevy
with tan upholstery. It has a spare key and a spare tire. She's
never had a flat. Never run out of gas. Her house is large and
everybody sleeps in beds. Her garden is for decoration with no

pit for burning trash. When she gets bored she talks about these
things and sometimes her college days, spent on the moon for
all I understand what she's talking about.

My uncle, who went to Indian school awhile and got left
behind. My uncle, kinder more decent certainly smarter and
more interesting than Miss Shawn. My brothers and sisters
who would have to have Miss Shawn for sixth grade after me.
My dad teaching us kids the most important word in the
Chippewa language, migwech. Indians. Chippewas. Visiting
joking laughing. My aunt setting her mother's hair.
    "*Nindaanis, are them pincurls good and tight?*"
    So tight, Ma, you won't be able to shut your eyes."
My cousin, who got slapped by his teacher for not speaking.
Timmy, the other Indian kid in class, getting slapped
by Miss Shawn for smiling during singing time. Miss Shawn.

I don't want to tell her.

Exposed, I look for shelter with a lie.

"Navajo."

"Oh. NAH vuh ho." Amazingly, she says
that I may sit down. And I have survived
unharmed, to take my place again behind
the boy who blocks her view of what I see.

It's not such a bad day at school, after all.

FOR ASIN

Eyes down sitting alone he is
below the salt outside the pale beyond the tracks
he is a twelfth grade Indian boy eating his lunch
on the steps outside the school.
His parents are proud his cousins envious
of the accomplishments of this invisible boy
this solitary warrior who is a silent apparition
unseen and unheard, unknown
by other students flirting and horsing around
on the steps after lunch unaware of the warrior,
those laughing girls in imported peasant chic
and teasing boys in jeans and chambray shirts,
the proletarian kitsch of 1973.
Eyes down he eats two vapor sandwiches
and folds the brown paper bag into his pocket
for tomorrow, then walks into school unnoticed,
a ghost floating past the guidance counselor's office.
This morning the ghost took human form
for the counselor, who with shortsighted eyes saw
an Indian boy head down too shy unappealing
frayed shirt bad teeth, a C student.

> *I was wondering about college, said the warrior.*
> *It isn't for everyone, said the counselor.*

Below the salt outside the pale beyond the tracks
unseen in silence the invisible warrior walks point.
He is a woodland warrior in a foreign jungle,
camouflaged in wash pants and frayed shirt,
a C student with bad teeth and downcast eyes
the pride of his parents the envy of his cousins
the hope of his brothers and sisters, walking point
leaving tracks the impossible shimmer of our dreams,
tracks that trace the shade of the sky the hue of tomorrow
through the foreign jungle across cracked concrete
up the stairs through the Age of Aquarius crowd
to college.

Asin, you walked before us.
Asin, in your memory and honor
we now rise to our feet and walk
step after step in your tracks
that we broaden to a path
the shade of the sky
the hue of tomorrow
the shimmer of your dreams.
Asin, in your memory and honor
visible now we walk.

THE CLASS OF 1968

Ten little, nine little, eight little Indians,
seven little, six little, five little Indians,
four little, three little, two little Indians,
one little Indian…

And that left me the last one
of the bunch, kindergarteners of 1955
our teachers our varied shades of skin our histories
those random chances silent banshees chasing children
one by one out of our parents' dreams til I was
the only one left, and the one perceived as leaving

leaving Vicky, pregnant in the eighth grade,
      who never came back
Vernon and George, nomads between res and town
      'til they were forgotten
Wanda, always sick and agonizingly shy, who disappeared
Birdeen, who went to work after her father died
Percy and John, expelled for fighting
and Susan for skipping school
      to take care of the younger kids at home
Jim, who studied incorrigibility at Juvenile Hall
Pete, who advanced that study at Red Wing
Eliza, who never learned to read
      and waited for her sixteenth birthday
Bonita, who almost made it but "had to" get married
      as we said in 1968

and that left me the last one
the forgotten the untouched the protected
the bookish the lucky the lonely
the last one.

LISA, LET US REMEMBER RICHARD

Do you remember Richard's hands, Lisa?
Michelangelo caught and stilled hands like Richard's,
his Adam's frescoed reach bound by two dimensions
that on Richard became four – height depth breadth time
   lives before us lives yet to come
   assailed existence onerous survival
   unregarded as art. Or beauty, although
   it is a beauty rougher than fresco
   and warm as wood, if wood were flesh
   elegantly crafted walnut with oil finish
delicately poised for work or rest and unaware
that surgeons, musicians, artists
would weep in envy at the sight

but there was more to this.
Richard's demeanor bespoke his hands
tentative, unobtrusive with a tremor ever so slight
that gave those hands an animation, life
that met and sang with the spirits who dwell
in pencils, spoons, split wood, rawhide.

Lisa, let us remember
the late summer afternoon
he sat on the back stairs making a drum.
We watched his hands hollow a stump
and stretch, coaxingly, wet rawhide
while my little girls and Richard's nieces
played on the swing set in the yard.
"Uncle Richard washed our hair last night,"
said Peaches. "For bugs; they're all gone now,"
said Kitty. Richard looked up and smiled as
those hands that had gently washed and combed
lice from little girls' hair shaped and smoothed
wet rawhide to a ragged circle, lacing top and bottom
back and forth, back and forth.

Do you see this photograph?
I walked among you with a roasting pan
of watermelon wedges that late summer day.

Out of the frame you stood by in a yellow apron, holding a
glass of red wine and looking upward. Was it cloud pictures
you saw of the last season's rice harvest, Richard newly sober
and newly strong; were you listening for the sky song of ricing
day? Braced against the car door he had danced on dried hulls.

While he carved a drumstick we sat on the back stairs
and watched the kids play. I recall damp wood and peeling
paint curving soft under our backsides, cool in the shade.

The drumstick carved and wrapped, he paused for coffee.
The dog, smitten by the smell of Richard and rawhide,
nosed and kissed his hands, and then slept at his feet.

Lisa, let us remember winter, that afternoon.
He changed the tire on my car, under a sun the color of clouds.
We stood close behind him to cut off the icy wet wind
"Makes me wish I had some gloves;
it's hard on the hands" he half-laughed in his quiet voice
as his fingers stiffened to hardwood from the wind
and the touch of that cold, cold iron jack.

Later on we walked along the tracks checking snares
        and I remember it like a photograph
        Richard in his red checked lumberjacket
        arms crossed, hands in his armpits
        you in your long dressy coat
        me in my mother's quilted jacket
and found a rabbit caught but still alive,
struggling it paused then kicked, paused then kicked
"I hate when this happens" Richard said
in his quiet voice, bending and turning away
to spare us the sight of what was necessary,
mercifully and quickly tightening the wire
with his kind and sorrowing hands.

At Richard's place, Donna made the soup
and fry bread so light it danced on the plate
(we didn't know a white girl could do that).
"What do you use, baking powder or soda?"
we aspiring Frybread Queens asked.
"I use both" said rosy Donna,
all bashful as an Indian.
"I taught her how" said Richard
as Donna charmed golden puffs from the stove.

Then, with warmed hands the color of Donna's bread
and rough and graceful as the old wood table we sat at
he served us all, his elderly father first.
Feasting, we listened to Richard's dad, veteran and elder
with Richard's distant, husky voice
tell us about when he was in the army,
stationed in the South years ago, after the Great War
and all the mixed-blood people down there.
"Good to us, the Makadewisug; always
nice to Indians, and fed us, too.
A lot of them part Indian themselves, you know;
treated us nice and shared their food with us."

In the spring Richard showed us how to cut porcupine quills
under a plastic bread wrapper, with toenail clippers
so the little points wouldn't fly up
and put out our eyes.
He made us quill necklaces light as air
that rested on our collarbones, singing his songs.

He wrote to me once after I moved away
on a card he'd bought specially,
with a sketch of an Indian woman on it
he hoped all was good and that I liked the picture

then he moved, too,
to Minneapolis, near the Ave,
and was lost

I ran into his sister after that
and she said I wouldn't know him if I saw him
that he was killing himself drinking

Liisi-ens, sometimes I do it, too,
step out of the frame and look skyward
where for all we know it is possible
that we might see Richard
in the clouds.

TO THE WOMAN WHO JUST BOUGHT THAT SET OF NATIVE AMERICAN SPIRITUALITY DREAM INTERPRETATION CARDS

Sister, listen carefully to this.
You'll probably go right past me
when you're looking
for a real   gen-yew-whine
Indian princess
to flagellate you deliciously
and feed your self-indulgent
un-guilt
about what other people
not as fine-tuned and sensitive as you
did to women
by the way, women like me
who you probably go right past
when you're looking.

I know what you're looking for
and that I'm not it.
You're looking for that other
Indian woman you want
a for real   gen-yew-whine
oshkii-traditional princess
and you'll know her when you see her
glibly glinting silver and turquoise
carrying around her own little
magic shop of real   gen-yew-whine
rattling beads and jangling charms
beaming about her moon
as she sells you a ticket to her sweat lodge.
She's a spiritual concession stand
and it's your own business go ahead and buy
or rent it if you want go ahead
acquire what you will,
you've done it before.
I know what you're looking for
and that I'm not it.   Hell.
I won't be dressing up or dancing for you
or selling you a ceremony
that women around here never even heard of
I won't tell your fortune
or interpret your dreams
so put away your money. Hell.

Sister, you weren't listening to this
I know, but I know too that
that authentic, guaranteed
satisfaction or your money back
gen-yew-whine for real
oshkii-traditional Indian princess
is easy to find. She takes cash
or credit cards, no checks.
Acquire what you will.
I'll be watching you both.

What you're looking for
you'll never see and anyway
it's not for sale.

Mary Susan

Our little sister was named after an aunt who died before we were born. Aunt Mary Susan was a young girl, a student at a South Dakota mission school near the Wounded Knee Massacre in 1890. The nuns at the school, hearing that something bad was going on, took the children out to a ditch where they spent the night. They survived.

Mary Susan returned to Minnesota, where she married, had five children and was widowed. Left with small children to support, she found a job as a cook at the Vermilion Lake Indian School, then spent all of her working years with boarding school children. My dad remembers her as a generous woman, only as tall as a child, who spoke softly and kindly. He honored her memory by naming our little sister after her.

Our little sister is the only blonde in our family. As children we were fascinated by her coloring, her hair that lightened to an ice frost in the summer, her cheeks that bloomed with a red fire in the winter. Winters she became the sun, summers the moon. We masked our anger and humiliation at the neighbors' stupid jokes about the stork, the wrong baby, the milkman by pretending we didn't understand. She was our sister, we could see that. We were photo negatives, reversals of the same black and white image, a bone structure and history interchangeable under skin, eyes and hair.

In the 1970s an Indian Club was started at our high school. What an event that was, an organization to acknowledge and reinforce Indian ways in an institution that had stood for the annihilation of our people through education/assimilation. Our little sister went to Indian Club until picture day, when the other students asked her to step off the riser and out of the camera's eye because with her coloring she wouldn't match the group on the yearbook page.

After that she always felt like she stood out in pictures.

Nindaaniss Waawashkeshikwesens On A Winter Night

In the moonlit quiet of a winter night

as I pass her bedroom door

Nindaaniss Waawaashkeshikwesens

my daughter the Deer Girl

springs from her bed.

From the distant dark forest of her sleep

she totters to my arms,

her wide dark eyes asking "What? Wegonen?"

and I carefully lead her back to her bed.

"My girl, shh, shh, nibaan, nibaan,

go to sleep, go back to sleep."

Folding her slender deer legs

she nestles under the pile of blankets

I tuck around her

and her wide dark eyes close

as she returns to the distant dark forest sleep

of the Waawaashkeshiwag.

MY DAD, WHO TREATS LIFE LIKE A SACRAMENT

He drank the whole glass down all at once

      with respect

      eyes closed

      no stopping

and said to me

"there's nothing like milk, my girl"

and I could see

cows and green grass and sunshine

beautiful children with white teeth

all that might be

the good life it was

a sacrament right there for the taking.

IV BIBOON WINTER

ANISHINAABIKWE - EVERYWOMAN

He Inini

    Native man who seeks the Great Spirit

    looks longingly out the window

        past the birds and trees

        into his own mind

    long hair hiding his back

I Ikwe

    Native woman so close to Mother Earth

    protect him from this cruel and mundane life

    hard work   courage   love

    my strengths

    while my feet never leave the ground.

My quest never began

and his will never end.

IKWE ISHPIMING

From black of light years, asi anang
writhed and spiraled into his path,
shedding sparks that dazzled his eyes.
He raised his arm to shade his face
and began his dance, unaware that he danced
while above I flew, gold in the sky.
With my hair the wind I tethered his wrists
to a shining cloud, as I silently swayed
and breathed in the wind, ambe, ambe.
My hands the earth that gave him life
bathed his feet in shredding silk
that tore in my touch as I whispered,
ambe omaa, bimosen, bimosen.
Then my lips rained silver sand that poured
into the river that rolled from its sleep
and I spoke through the water, wewiib, wewiib,
til he followed, filling my tracks with his own.

Casualty Days

Back here in the world as summer passed
through bright and gritty dog days, tethered girls
captured faceless voices and placed calls
linking braided coiled color snakes
red white grey white across the continent,
    Sharon to Missoula, Pam to New York
their sad and tender fingers glittering
in the absence of their men who slept, it seemed
to the girls on second shift it almost seemed
they slept near the China Sea.

I passed them on the sidewalk outside Bell,
some college kids home on their summer break,
girls in hippie dress and peasant chic
boys in blue chambray work shirts and jeans
assumed innocence sitting cross-legged
(Indian-style, they thought) on the sidewalk
singing and chanting "*Ho Ho Ho Chi Minh*!
NLF is gonna win!" A white girl
costumed ersatz Indian princess
who wore a beaded headband from Japan
looked right through me, a Native working girl
in a shirtwaist dress, carrying a vinyl purse.

Upstairs we plaited spiderwebs of calls.
"*Solidarity forever; our union makes us free*"
floated up on humid summer hair
to our window and over the switchboard
weighting the hands and hearts of anchored girls,
unseen sisters of the working class.

And sleepless girls we sang through the night
songs I remember as I remember our fright
    Operator.
    Your number please?
    Please deposit ten cents more.
    Operator.
    Your number please?
    I'm sorry, ma'am, your time is up.

Remember, Bev, how very young we were?
I remember, and remember how he'd kissed your pretty face.
I remember your blue eyes and waiting face.

And Bev, remember those "Casual Wear Days"
when operators who met their quotas
were rewarded with pot luck lunches
and freed from polyester working clothes
for a day of being someone not ourselves?
In jeans, we almost looked like college girls.

That summer day you maintained,
sweatered chilled fragile gratefully talking
recipes with the older operators,
kind ladies their spreading flesh fading and
Tussy-scented within their casual wear,
picnic "wash" dresses soft with wear and age.
Polite and frightened we spooned and swallowed
uneasy noodle salads, their intended comforts
our reward for being such good and grownup girls.

Remembering themselves in other wars
theyknew; they knew how young we really were

Summer passed; days shortened and grew cold.
Migratory birds and college kids
soared and disappeared into the sky.

Here in the world we hurried to work
in thin-soled flats light on the frosty sidewalk
to punch in and anchor to the switchboard,
bound and faceless girls weaving America
red white grey white across the continent
Duluth to Detroit, to the fire department
to the Busy Bee Market. Business. Births. Deaths.

Bev, that January casual wear day
you maintained, pale and thin in winter white.
Below the bowl held out on the palm of your left hand
your diamond ring, loose, spun and caught the light.
That day, white marble balanced on an egg
as flatly jazzed bridal lasagna sweat
uneasy beads through wedding gift Pyrex embellished
with gold roosters flaunting avocado plumes
while shivering girls tiptoed through their bloom.

Pammy's cave rat trapped deep in the jungle,
and Sharon's sniper in that twelve-foot boat,
in sleep, those absent boys, what did they dream
while their feet softened and yellowed, damp
in heavy laced boots, near the China Sea?
And your own soldier, Bev, lost there in the fog
within the greenest of jungles, woke dreaming of you.

Remember, Bev, how very young we were?
I remember, and remember how he'd kissed your pretty face.

PARTURITION, A POEM FOR BRENDA AND TERRIE

Having won the game of patience seven times

    and lost four

I re-rubberband the deck

    my legs writhe restlessly, straighten

and rise wobbily to stand on dusty gray linoleum,

    soles balance my weight, my soul my wait

which pleases the labor room nurse (she who holds all power)

    "Look how limber she is! Jumped right off that bed!
    Good idea, walk...walk...that'll get that baby out.
    Ring if you need me!"

from a great distance it seems

    she bubbles through waves, and waves

thus grounded perhaps in control of my destiny,
the sullen indignities of these hours cumbrous
on my unseen feet yellow with cold I imagine
that walk a crescent fertile and horseshoe-shaped
around the bed and back, around and back;
above, my yet unbirthed motherspirit
listens to seasounds from the swimmer within.

After countless paced crescents she startles me,
an old woman with lined elm bark face and calm eyes
watching me through a small window in the wall

    "Grandmother? " I wonder, heartened
    by this visit I have wished for in my dreams
    since the day she died two months
    into my own conception

then realize the window is a mirror,
and I an ageless crone at twenty-two.

In that dimension past where numbers end
but not this walk and wait, yoked to this time
and clutching to each hip a fabric bouquet
blue fleur-de-lis on a tattered hospital gown
barefoot left crescent turn right crescent turn
as the waves crest break recede, crest break recede

and halt, silence.

    Where are the seasounds?

I have worn a shining silver omega
that frames the bed, gray linoleum buffed
and polished by my blessedly pain-free feet
that now step cautiously past my cronehood
and syncopate dustily toward my husband,
who sleeps in a harvest gold vinyl chair with chrome legs

    "Can you hear that?" I inhale to form the words
    "I can't hear the seasounds anymore."

but in that breath the swimmer turns, the silence breaks
with a pop as water rushes, flooding my cold yellow feet
with warm waves that carry dust bunnies
from beneath the bed to the corners of the room
out the door and down the corridor
to the nurse's station.
I complete my inhalation. Should I ring?

    "Did you hear something?" my husband asks
    through the pitch of the rippling sea
    "Did you hear something?" he asks the girl I used to be

The Beanbag

When the snow began to thaw, at first we saw
only a trace of flowered calico,
then every day more cotton flowers bloomed,
deep blue blossoms wet with melting snow.
Familiar, it looked. I remembered
forget-me-nots on her favorite house dress
that, when worn out, she crocheted with a hook
into a rug, mostly; the smallest scrap
she sewed into a child's toy, a beanbag.

I remember that dress.
As a child, when she held me close,
my face against her soft, flowered middle
smelling starch and warm geranium
in her soft and cool fleshy embrace
I felt small, an infant, or not yet
born in a cocoon of blue flowered cloth.

Early in spring after she died
one day I recognized that flowered dress:
forget-me-nots on cotton, wet buds of blue flowers
on a beanbag we were kicking around the yard.

Split, it spilled the past

> her kitchen floor
> bumpy patterned linoleum, shiny and bare
> reflecting wavy geraniums in coffee cans,
> nurtured from seeds of their own great-grandmothers

> checked oilcloth
> leaned to white pearl scallops at the edge
> by her daughters' slender, bending waists
> and ground to silver dollars, several pairs,
> by her ravenous sons' elbows

> kitchen woodstove a hot dull black
> bread baking in the oven;
> above, noodles boiling tomatoes roiling
> singing huffs of steam above our heads

I remembered when the beanbag spilled the past;
when it split and spilled the past I remembered,
and picked it up, to see it one more time

and what was that? I looked close, and closer.
Through its frayed weave, of returning to the earth
the bag held life beyond the tiny past.
Split and spilt, its damp side finely pierced
by an infant bean seedling yet blind, but greedy
for the light, born in a cocoon of flowered
blue calico, a pattern wet with snow
forget-me-nots an early sign of spring
entwined now with a trace of tender green.

I remember her flowered dress.
That dress.

Looking for a Woman with the Blues

he was looking for a woman with the blues
the blue blue blues of a woman wronged
so blue in the glass we sang our sad songs
while he picked up his guitar and strummed along

he drove in behind a bucking bronc, defeat
in rusting mirrored triumph strutting
bravado offerings of self-loathing, free lunch
for sad women in a dark and noisy bar, while she

grieving past competition won hands down,
a doe downed gutted consumed by fire
ashes blown across blackened, ice-bound ruins
dusty rose lace curtains, ruffled in the snow

then banshee clouds tattooed by purple thumbs
broke to women swimming up in smoke
that tasted of the hot blue fires of hell
but the winner was the saddest of us all

he'd found himself a woman with the blues

SETTING BAIT FOR THE TRICKSTER

women bring him things

bits of paper with little notes

coffee mugs hip clever (sneakily) domestic

dead mice from the field

we can't help our nature

we'd catch him if we could

but we can't

nevertheless

we leave small corpses

 hopeful offerings

at the doorstep

E.W. Bohannon, My Grandmother, and Me

E.W. Bohannon rests upright under glass,
blind blue gaze dignified and detached, calmly
afloat on a pale sea, enigmatic` doldrums
of cured beiges contoured on a flat stretched canvas.

More often than I should I pause here,
my rushed steps down this tiled and wax-dusted hall
slowed and drawn to the painterly portrait
of this long-dead educator
> and my own superimposed reflection,
> shadowed palimpsest that traces a third face
> silent planes of my own grandmother's
> whose years (and her children's)
> at boarding schools
> *Red Lake Mission; Tomah; Hayward;*
> *Vermilion Lake; Red Lake Government*
> coincided with E.W.'s tenure and now
> collide in the layering of countenances

pondering his academic gown hood demeanor
and his civilized world of books and order
preserved in an oil now dry
and fragile as his flesh and bones
long moldered to powder underground
in darkness to dust.

The brass plate at the bottom of the portrait

> Eugene William Bohannon
> President, Duluth State Teachers College
> 1901-1938

is a small grave marker in a toy cemetery,
a headstone at the foot of a canvas imitation
of life forgotten for a half-century
while the world beyond the vault
reinvented itself history repeating history,
the robed and seated scholar shrouded
indefinitely in brown paper secured by twine
as he waited as Wells' time traveler
for the machine to halt and tip him sideways
into the endless argument over what is light
and what dark; what is Eloi and what is Morlock.

Since his resurrection, E.W. has seen the light
of day only, in the building that bears his name
in this dreamlike portrait, painted
in what looks like the most civilized of times.
From behind glass he blinks slowly, through the reflection
of my grandmother's eyes at this loiterer I am,
who pauses more often than she should at this case
to wonder, to ponder the parallel worlds
between his existence her grandmother's and her own,
attempting and failing to reconcile today with the past.

Fearlessly – I hope - we stare him down,
my grandmother's shadow and I,
without expression we blink slowly back at E.W. Bohannon,
displayed under glass.

Magdalene in the Shade of Veronica's Love

She kneels, covering his feet with her long hair,
this young and ruined woman weeping her regrets.

He takes her hand and she rises, forgiven;
the repentant beauty of her face fills his eyes.

So long ago, before time mortified my soul
I begged strangers for an imprint
that their hands their lips might mark my existence,
this now manifest in the inconsequentiality
of cronehood, the lines of my face
the whiteness of my hair
my mottled hands misshapen fingers.

Where is the absolution
for the inconsequential spirit?

Within the void that is the crowd
my hands ache curve like claws
touch no one nothing
but the reluctant sorrowful mystery.

Shame and salvation.
I would gather her pain
to my betrayed and tender waste.
I would weep if I could but can only sway
above this disarming, guileless grief.

MIGWECHIWENDAM OJIBWEMOWIN

O'o apii ninganawaamabamaag noozhishshenyyag,
ingiw minawaanigwe'odeg,
nimiigwechniwendam.

Onaangi wii'awensiwaan
gaye ozide'iwaan naanimiwag
amanj igo api mawadishiwewaad
omishomisimiwaa gaye ookomisimiwaa owaakaa'iganiwag.
Ninzaagitoon oninjiwan
    iniw oninjiiniwaan nimbi-biidamawigoog
    wenizhishid asin
    misko'ode ziizibaakwadoonsan
    gikinjigwewin
    zoomiingweniwin gaye bozagozid ojiimewin.

Ninzhawendaagoz.

Ayaangodinong nimaaminowendam komisag.
Mewinzha giigozi ishpiming
nasaab noongoom megwe'oog niinawin.
O'o apii ninganawaabamaag noozhishenhyag
nimaaminonendaanan gete gizhigoon gaye noongoom,
noongoom gaye waabang gaye awas-waabang,
mii dash ningikwendam
ninzhaawendaagoz ikweyaan, niin.

Mi dash ni migwechiwendam.

Migwech, dash minawaa migwech.

Migwechiwendam Shaaganaashimowin

When I look at my grandchildren,
those sweet and happy hearts,
I think with gratitude.

Their bodies are small and light,
and their little feet dance
when they visit
at their grandpa's and grandma's house.
I love their small hands
that bring to me
> a pretty rock
> red heart candy
> a hug
> a smile and a sticky kiss.

I am fortunate.

Sometimes
I think about my grandmothers.
A long time ago they went to live in heaven,
yet they are still at this same time among us.
When I look at my grandchildren
I consider the old days and the present,
today and tomorrow and the day after tomorrow,
and then I know
that I am blessed, a fortunate woman.

And I think with gratitude.

Migwech, and again migwech.

and today, Wazhashk, hear us breathe
a continuing song
a continuing song
since long before the memory of mortals

BINI is set in Palatino, a twentieth century font designed by Hermann Zapf based on the humanist typefaces of the Italian Renaissance and named for the sixteenth century Italian master of calligraphy Giambattista Palatino.